Benjamin Franklin

A Boy of Invention

The Franklin family lived in Boston, Massachusetts. Ben was born in 1706. He had sixteen brothers and sisters. At that time our country was still a colony—a part of England. As Benjamin grew, so did the country.

FRANKLIN'S BIRTHPLACE.

Ben went to school for only two years. He learned to read and write there. After that, he taught himself many things. Ben had big ideas about how things worked.

When Ben was a man, he did experiments with lightning using a kite and a key.

When Ben was twelve years old, his brother James taught him how to be a printer. Ben learned all about printing newspapers.

FRANKLIN,

THE APPRENTICE BOY.

NEW YORK:

HARPER & BROTHERS, PUBLISHERS.

Title page of a book about Franklin

Young Benjamin at work

A Young Man of Letters

Ben played a trick on his brother. He wrote letters to his brother's newspaper and signed the letters "Silence Dogood." Many people liked reading the letters in the newspaper, but James was not happy. When he found out Ben had written the letters, he was angry.

Franklin, far right, working for his brother

When Ben was seventeen he went to Philadelphia to find work. Ben worked for printing houses in Philadelphia and in London, England. He was bursting with new ideas and opened his own print shop in Philadelphia. He printed a book each year called *Poor Richard's Almanack.* The book was filled with weather forecasts, advice, and wise sayings.

Franklin started his own print shop. He used a pen name when he wrote *Poor Richard's Almanack.*

Poor Richard, 1733.

AN

Almanack

For the Year of Chrift

1733,

Being the Firft after LEAP YEAR:

And makes fince the Creation	Years
By the Account of the Eaftern *Greeks*	7241
By the Latin Church, when ☉ ent. ♈	6932
By the Computation of *W. W.*	5742
By the *Roman* Chronology	5682
By the *Jewifh* Rabbies	5494

Wherein is contained

The Lunations, Eclipfes, Judgment of the Weather, Spring Tides, Planets Motions & mutual Afpects, Sun and Moon's Rifing and Setting, Length of Days, Time of High Water, Fairs, Courts, and obfervable Days.

Fitted to the Latitude of Forty Degrees, and a Meridian of Five Hours Weft from *London*, but may without fenfible Error, ferve all the adjacent Places, even from *Newfoundland* to *South-Carolina*.

By *RICHARD SAUNDERS*, Philom.

PHILADELPHIA:
Printed and fold by *B. FRANKLIN*, at the New Printing-Office near the Market.

Ben arrived in Philadelphia with little money.

Ben the Inventor

Ben had ideas to help people. Fires were very common in cities like Philadelphia. The fires burned many houses. Ben's idea was to set up a fire department.

One artist painted Ben as a firefighter.

Ben Franklin even invented a way to make better use of fire. He created a metal stove that fit inside a fireplace.

Franklin's design for a stove

The Franklin stove used less wood and threw more heat into a room.

Ben got tired of switching to reading glasses every time he had something to read. So he cut his lenses in half. He put the reading lenses together with regular lenses in one frame.

Franklin invented bifocals.

A National Leader

Many people thought England's rules were unfair. Ben and other leaders wrote their ideas in the Declaration of Independence. They asked the king of England to let the colonies have a say in making rules.

The Declaration of Independence committee, with Franklin at the far left

Franklin presenting the Declaration of Independence

The Declaration led to war between England and the colonies. The colonies needed help to win. Ben had an idea! At 70 years old, Ben sailed across the Atlantic Ocean to ask France for help in the war.

Benjamin Franklin meeting the king and queen of France

At age 84 Ben Franklin died. His inventions, writings, and many of his good ideas live on today.

Let's Explore!

This map shows Philadelphia when Benjamin Franklin lived there. Tell how Franklin could travel from his house to Independence Hall.

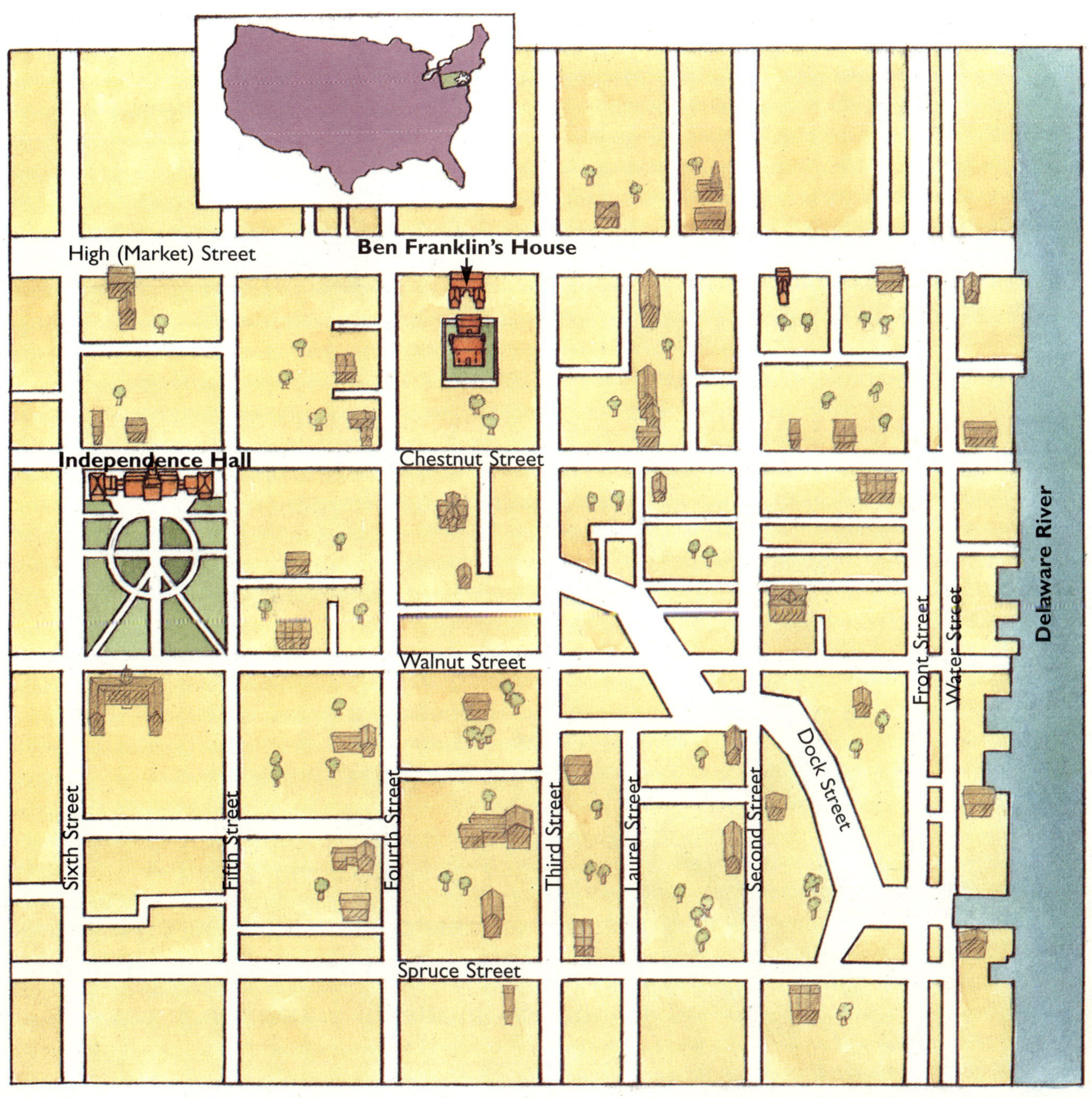

What Do You Think?

BIG IDEAS

Do you have a big idea you think would help others? Share your idea in pictures and words. Your big idea might be a new way to do something that saves time or effort, or it might be a way to solve arguments among your friends.

NO PROBLEM

With a friend, role-play being Ben Franklin and a young friend who has a problem. Tell "Ben" what the problem is, such as your house is cold or you can't read the newspaper. "Ben" tells how to solve the problem.

A FRANKLIN MONUMENT

Benjamin Franklin's picture appears on money and stamps. Think of a monument for him. Tell where you would build it. Then draw a picture or build a model of your monument.

BEN'S SIGNATURE

Benjamin Franklin signed all four of these documents: the Declaration of Independence, the Treaty of Alliance, the Treaty of Paris, and the Constitution of the United States.

Declaration of Independence	Treaty of Alliance	Treaty of Paris	Constitution of the United States
Document that gave the reasons why the colonists wanted their independence	**Agreement between France and the colonists**	**Agreement that ended the war with England**	**Document that described how the new United States government would work**

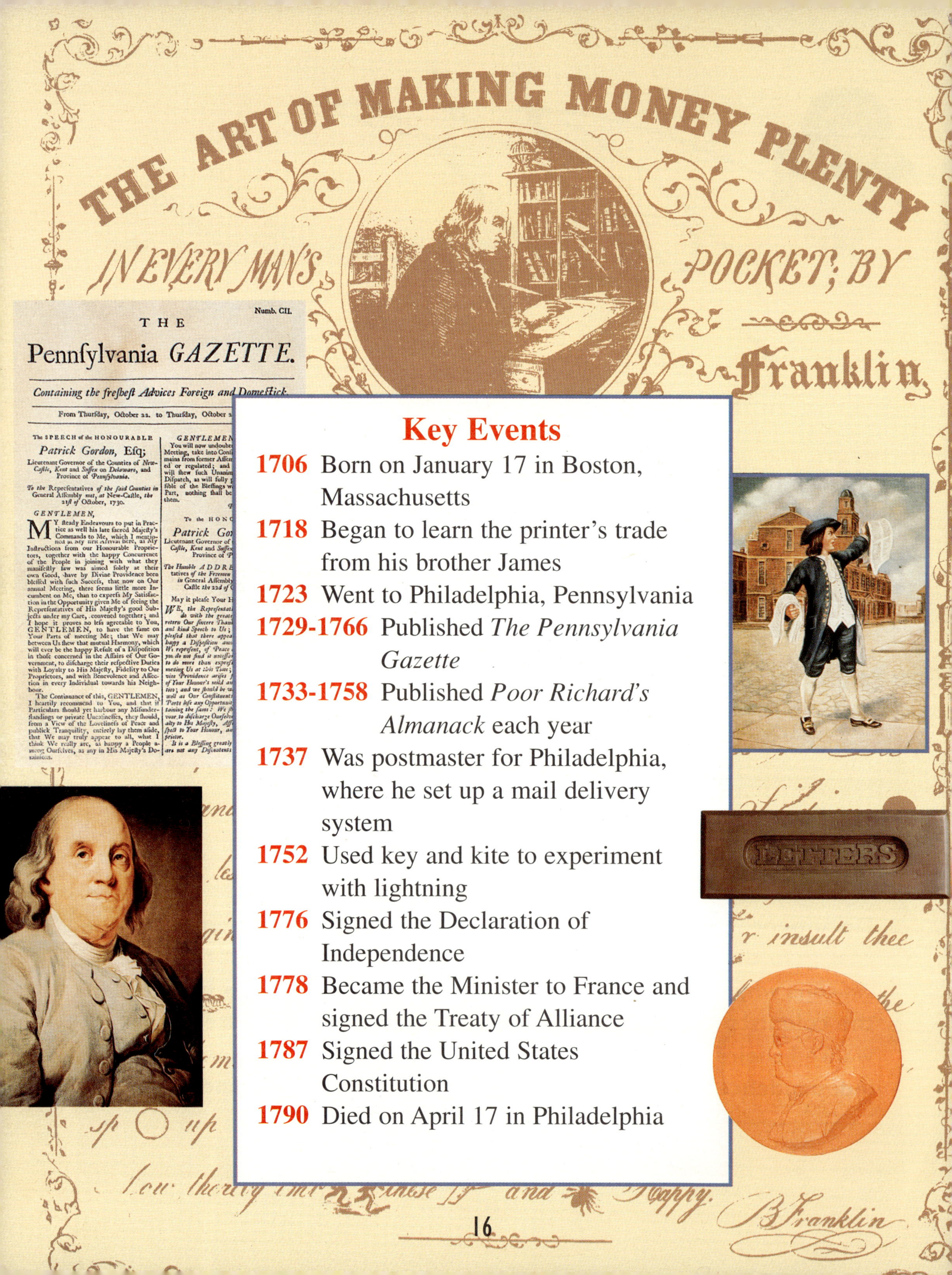

Key Events

1706 Born on January 17 in Boston, Massachusetts

1718 Began to learn the printer's trade from his brother James

1723 Went to Philadelphia, Pennsylvania

1729-1766 Published *The Pennsylvania Gazette*

1733-1758 Published *Poor Richard's Almanack* each year

1737 Was postmaster for Philadelphia, where he set up a mail delivery system

1752 Used key and kite to experiment with lightning

1776 Signed the Declaration of Independence

1778 Became the Minister to France and signed the Treaty of Alliance

1787 Signed the United States Constitution

1790 Died on April 17 in Philadelphia